ACAI SUPER BERRY

COOKBOOK

Inspiring | Educating | Creating | Entertaining

Brimming with creative inspiration, how-to projects, and useful information to enrich your everyday life, Quarto Knows is a favorite destination for those pursuing their interests and passions. Visit our site and dig deeper with our books into your area of interest: Quarto Creates, Quarto Cooks, Quarto Homes, Quarto Lives, Quarto Drives, Quarto Explores, Quarto Gifts, or Quarto Kids.

ISBN: 978-1-57715-189-0

Editorial Director: Rage Kindelsperger
Creative Director: Laura Drew
Managing Editor: Cara Donaldson
Senior Editor: John Foster
Interior Design: Evelin Kasikov
All photography © Shutterstock

Printed in China

This book provides general information. It should not be relied upon as recommending or promoting any specific diagnosis or method of treatment for a particular condition, and it is not intended as a substitute for medical advice or for direct diagnosis and treatment of a medical condition by a qualified physician. Readers who have questions about a particular condition, possible treatments for that condition, or possible reactions from the condition or its treatment should consult a physician or other qualified health care professional.

MIX
Paper from
responsible sources
FSC® C016973
www.fsc.org

ACAI SUPER BERRY
COOKBOOK

**Over 50
Natural and Healthy
Smoothie, Bowl, and
Sweet Treat
Recipes**

Melissa Petitto, R. D.

WELLFLEET
PRESS

INTRODUCTION

A species of the palm tree, the acai palm, is cultivated for the acai berry and hearts of palm. The word *acai* literally means "fruit that cries," or fruit that expels water. It is a berry that rapidly ferments, and because of this we typically find it in dried powder form and frozen puree form.

This berry is native to Brazil, Trinidad, and other countries in northern South America. Mainly growing in swamps and floodplains, it has been a staple of the Ribeirinhos people for thousands of years. There are so many unique descriptions of its flavor: not sweet like a typical berry, bitter, chocolaty aftertaste, earthy, rich, and milky. I think this is why it lends itself so wonderfully to smoothies and smoothie bowls, because it is a berry of many flavor profiles.

Its popularity has grown tremendously with the current focus on healthy eating. Although acai has been a staple food in the Amazon River delta, its source of energy replacement and "superfood" qualities have recently made it a staple in health and nutrition stores and restaurants. It is said that a family of martial artists included it in puree form for training athletes, and then it began to appear on menus in Rio as an ice cream-like treat. Acai was pretty unknown until two Californian surfing brothers were wowed by its energy-boosting properties and found a way to import the frozen stuff to North America.

Its nutrition breakdown is quite remarkable. In its frozen form, 3.5 ounces (100 g) has 247 calories, and acai has higher antioxidant levels than blueberries. In its freeze-dried form, 1.75 ounces (50 g) has 265 calories, 26 grams of carbohydrates, 4 grams of protein, and 16 grams of fat, mostly stemming form oleic acid and monounsaturated fat. The powdered form is particularly rich in calcium and vitamin A. This tiny berry also offers the highest phytochemical content of any fruit or vegetable. These phytochemicals, especially anthocyanin and phenolic acid, are plant compounds that offer disease-fighting properties that benefit our health in many different ways. Let's chat about why the acai berry is so incredibly healthy.

Nutrient dense: The acai berry is unique for a fruit. It is high in good fats and low in sugar.

Antioxidant load: The acai berry is loaded with antioxidants. The oxygen radical absorbance capacity (ORAC) score typically measures the antioxidant levels of foods. Just 3.5 ounces (100 g) of acai pulp has an ORAC score of 15,405, whereas the blueberry has a score of 4,669 for the same amount. Specifically, the antioxidant anthocyanin may lower oxidative stress and inflammation, promoting brain health. Anthocyanins have been shown to not only enhance but also improve memory, reduce the risk of heart attacks in young and middle-aged women, and aid in anticancer activities.

Brain function: We've touched on how the acai berry may improve brain function, but it definitely deserves a little more attention. Many studies have been done on how the antioxidant in acai, anthocyanin, counteracts the detrimental effects of inflammation and oxidation on brain cells. This inflammation negatively affects memory and learning processes. One of the main ways that acai has been shown to help with brain function is in its ability to "clean house." As our brain ages, the process of cleaning up the toxic brain cells that are no longer working properly, known as autophagy, is slowed down and less efficient. However, acai extract helps stimulate this neuronal housekeeping function.

Anticancer: No one food has the ability to stop cancer, but some superfoods have been shown to have anticancer properties. Acai has demonstrated great potential in this area due to its high antioxidant levels.

Cholesterol levels: Studies have shown that the regular consumption of acai pulp can help lower blood cholesterol levels and decrease the chances of heart disease by decreasing LDL, or "bad," cholesterol and improving HDL, or "good," cholesterol.

Skin health: Acai is being used in beauty products because of its high antioxidant levels. But the fruit is not only topically beneficial: eating acai berries is incredible for increasing skin density and promoting that natural glow we all crave.

Superfood is a term thrown around a lot in our vocabulary lately. What is a superfood and how is acai one? Superfood is a nonmedical term that has been popularized by the media. It refers to foods that have great health-promoting properties due to their high levels of antioxidants, vitamins, or other nutrients that have been shown to reduce the risk for disease and improve physical or emotional health. Acai is considered a superfood because it has super-high levels of antioxidants and helps reduce the risk of heart disease and cancer, lowers LDL cholesterol, and improves brain function.

How can you use acai in your diet? Acai comes in two main forms: as a frozen pulp (puree) in 3.5-ounce (100-g) packets and as a powder. The frozen pulp is excellent for smoothies, smoothie bowls, ice pops, sorbets, gelato, frozen yogurt, iced tea, and granitas. The powdered form is great in sweet treats such as brownies, muffins, cupcakes, fudge, granola, waffles, energy balls, and pancakes.

In this book, I have broken down our use of acai into three main sections. I've started with smoothies, then smoothie bowls, and then miscellaneous sweet treats. Not only have I included acai in every single recipe, but I have also added other incredible superfoods, including chia seeds, spirulina, baobab, cacao, and maca. These other superfoods can be left out, but they do make each recipe unique and highly nutritious.

Here is a list of the superfoods that I have included in this book, and if I've found an amazing source, I have included that as well. Always store these superfoods in a cool, dark, dry place to prevent spoilage.

 1. Chia seeds: High in omega-3 fatty acids and fiber, chia seeds are also a good source of calcium, potassium, and copper. Buy chia seeds in their whole seed form, not ground.

 2. Unsweetened coconut flakes: Coconut is high in omega-3 fatty acids, fiber, phosphorus, and iron. Buy unsweetened coconut.

3. Turmeric: This incredible spice contains a powerful compound called curcumin, which is anti-inflammatory, aids digestion, fights cancer, eases arthritis, and lowers the risk of heart attacks. Certified organic turmeric is best; avoid powder with any additives and fillers. This ensures that the turmeric is of the highest quality and has the greatest curcumin content.

 4. Maca: This powerful compound contains eight essential amino acids, fatty acids, calcium, magnesium, iron, and potassium. It is also a great hormone-balancing substance. When buying maca powder, always choose organic maca root. My favorite brand is Healthworks Maca Powder Peruvian Raw Organic.

 5. Cacao: This superfood is rich in flavonoids, decreases LDL cholesterol, increases HDL cholesterol, reduces inflammation, and improves blood sugar levels. Always buy organic, unsweetened cacao. One of the best sources is cacao nibs.

 6. Ginger root: This powerful root is anti-inflammatory, helps regulate blood sugar, and relieves gastrointestinal distress. You can buy this in pure root form, peel it, and add it to smoothies, or buy it in organic powdered form.

 7. Moringa: This nutrient powerhouse contains twenty-five times more iron than spinach and is a great source of zinc and magnesium. Always buy organic moringa leaf powder. Some of my favorite brands are Pura Vida, Organic Veda, Maju Superfoods, and Only Natural.

8. Camu camu: This berry has a potent punch of vitamin C; 1 teaspoon provides 118 percent of the daily recommended intake. Terrasoul Superfoods and Kiva Organics make two of my favorite products.

9. Mangosteen: This superfood is high in fiber, low in calories, and has a good serving of vitamin C, magnesium, and potassium. It also contains major cancer-fighting agents. When buying mangosteen, always buy organic. My favorite brand is Terrasoul Superfoods.

10. Matcha: This tea is full of catechins, an antioxidant that has been shown to help fight and possibly prevent cancer. This compound has a rich spring green color and is always best when purchased organic. A couple of my favorite brands are Encha Matcha, Pure Matcha, and Mizuba Tea Matcha.

11. Cayenne: This spice is rich in potassium, manganese, flavonoids, and vitamins C, B6, and E. Cayenne has been shown to ease an upset stomach, ulcers, sore throats, coughs, and diarrhea. It is also a great digestive aid.

12. Almonds: This nut has natural calming properties, as it is rich in stress-reducing vitamins and minerals like magnesium, zinc, and vitamin E. For the smoothie and smoothie bowl recipes in this book, always purchase organic raw almonds.

13. Cardamom: This spice is a great source of potassium, calcium, and magnesium and contains volatile oils, such as pinene, sabinene, myrcene, phellandrene, and limonene, all of which aid digestion, making this spice an excellent addition to your smoothies, smoothie bowls, and baked goods. Always buy organic high-quality cardamom.

14. Baobab: This antioxidant-rich superfood is very high in vitamin C, which helps in the production of collagen and elastin. Calcium, copper, iron, magnesium, and potassium are all contained in baobab. My favorite brand of baobab is Kaibae, which is superior in quality and also gives back to the farmers producing it.

I am almost ready to set you free into the world of acai deliciousness, but first I want to talk about substitutions for these recipes. I believe in the power of plants, and that is shown in my love of plant-based milks and yogurts in each of these recipes. However, feel free to swap them out for Greek yogurt or cow's milk if you prefer.

PART I

Smoothies

Chia Seed, Acai, and Berry Smoothie

SERVES 2

This smoothie packs an extra punch of omega-3s and fiber from the chia seeds. These little seeds, which have been cultivated since the time of the Aztecs, contain 10 grams of fiber, 5 grams of protein, and a good dose of calcium, potassium, and copper in 1 ounce (28 g). These powerhouses keep you full on only a few calories, making them a great weight-loss aid.

INGREDIENTS

7 ounces (200 g) frozen, unsweetened acai puree

2 tablespoons (14 g) chia seeds

2 cups (470 ml) unsweetened vanilla-flavored almond milk

1 frozen banana, peeled

1 cup (150 g) frozen organic mixed berries

1 tablespoon (20 g) raw local honey

2 tablespoons (20 g) granola

TIP

The best way to store chia seeds is in a glass mason jar with a tight-fitting lid in the refrigerator.

METHOD OF PREPARATION

Add the ingredients (except the granola) in the order listed to a high-powered blender. Puree until thick and creamy. Garnish with the granola if desired, and serve immediately.

Moringa, Acai, Blackberry, and Mint Smoothie

SERVES

This smoothie is not only a delicious combination of flavors, but it also contains a special powerhouse ingredient called moringa. This superfood has been used for anemia, arthritis and other joint pain, asthma, constipation, diabetes, diarrhea, stomach pain, fluid retention, and bacterial, fungal, viral, and parasitic infections. Basically, this plant is an antioxidant wonder food and it makes this smoothie extra special. You can add it to any and all smoothies!

INGREDIENTS

7 ounces (200 g) frozen, unsweetened acai puree

2 cups (300 g) frozen organic blackberries

2 cups (470 ml) coconut water

1 frozen banana, peeled

¼ cup (8 g) fresh organic mint leaves

1 tablespoon (8 g) moringa powder

1 tablespoon (20 g) raw local honey

TRY THIS!

Vibrant Skin Moringa Face Mask

½ tablespoon (4 g) moringa powder
1 teaspoon raw honey
1 teaspoon rose water
½ teaspoon fresh lemon juice
2 drops tea tree oil
↓
Mix together.
↓
Leave on face
for 10 to 15 minutes.

METHOD OF PREPARATION

Add the ingredients in the order listed to a high-powered blender. Puree until thick and creamy. Garnish with extra berries and a mint sprig if desired and serve immediately.

Omega-3 Coconut Smoothie

SERVES

This creamy smoothie is super coconutty amazingness! Its combination of acai, fig, and coconut in three different forms make it a great source of omega-3s and fiber. Just make sure you buy unsweetened coconut flakes, as the added sugar in sweetened coconut is not needed here.

TIP

Fresh figs are one of the most perishable produce items. They keep best when stored on a paper towel–lined shallow container in the refrigerator.

INGREDIENTS

7 ounces (200 g) frozen, unsweetened acai puree

10 fresh figs, quartered

1 cup (235 ml) coconut milk

1 cup (235 ml) coconut water

¼ cup (20 g) unsweetened coconut flakes

2 tablespoons (40 g) raw local honey

½ cup (75 g) ice cubes

METHOD OF PREPARATION

Add the ingredients in the order listed to a high-powered blender. Puree until thick and creamy. Rim the glass with coconut shavings for extra flavor. Serve immediately.

Antiviral Mango, Spinach, and Acai Smoothie

SERVES 👯

This smoothie contains the superfood camu camu. One spoonful of camu camu powder packs 118 percent of your recommended daily intake of vitamin C! This incredible superfood is also an antiviral, making it an excellent choice for people with cold sores, herpes, shingles, and even the common cold.

INGREDIENTS

7 ounces (200 g) frozen, unsweetened acai puree

4 Medjool dates, pitted

½ cup (120 ml) unsweetened almond or cashew milk

1 cup (235 ml) fresh orange juice

1 cup (85 g) frozen mango chunks

1 cup (30 g) fresh baby spinach

1 tablespoon (8 g) camu camu powder

½ cup (75 g) ice cubes

TIP
Camu camu oil has been shown to promote hair growth and guard against hair loss.

METHOD OF PREPARATION

Add the ingredients in the order listed to a high-powered blender. Puree until thick and creamy. Serve immediately.

Dark Chocolate, Acai, and Coffee Smoothie

SERVES 2

This smoothie is a perfect way to start the morning: think of it as a superfood chocolate coffee beverage! Cold-brewed coffee is far less acidic than coffee brewed hot, giving it a sweeter taste because of its lower acidity. Coffee contains many phytochemicals, antioxidants, and other nutrients that our bodies find beneficial. Its greater alkalinity makes this coffee beverage an excellent start to the day with less chance for acid reflux. Cold-brewed coffee is available in the refrigerated section of most grocery stores or can be brewed by steeping coarse-ground coffee beans in a coffee filter, cheesecloth, or nut milk bag overnight or up to 12 hours. It does take a long time to steep, so make a big batch and store it in the refrigerator for easy access.

INGREDIENTS

3.5 ounces (100 g) frozen, unsweetened acai puree

2 medium frozen bananas, peeled

1½ cups (355 ml) cold-brewed coffee

1 cup (235 ml) chocolate almond milk

2 tablespoons (30 g) peanut butter

2 tablespoons (16 g) unsweetened dark cacao powder

METHOD OF PREPARATION

Add the ingredients in the order listed to a high-powered blender. Puree until thick and creamy. Serve immediately. Mint garnish optional.

TIP

Let your bananas get super ripe and then peel and keep them in a freezer storage bag for easy smoothie making!

Anti-inflammatory Cherry, Acai, and Turmeric Smoothie

SERVES 2

This super smoothie is a powerful anti-inflammatory combination. Turmeric contains curcumin, which not only eases inflammation but also aids digestion, helps fight cancer, eases arthritis, and lowers the risk of heart attack. Turmeric has also been shown to help protect the brain with a compound known as ar-turmerone. This potent compound helps repair the brain's stem cells to keep the brain functioning at peak performance.

INGREDIENTS

7 ounces (200 g) frozen, unsweetened acai puree

1 medium frozen banana, peeled

2 scoops supergreens powder

1 cup (235 ml) black cherry juice

1 cup (150 g) frozen organic cherries

Juice of ½ lime

1 teaspoon turmeric

TIP

Amazing Grass brand makes an incredible supergreens product.

METHOD OF PREPARATION

Add the ingredients in the order listed to a high-powered blender. Puree until thick and creamy. Serve immediately. Garnish optional.

Avocado, Cashew, Spinach, and Acai Smoothie

SERVES

This creamy smoothie gets its monounsaturated fatty acids from the cashew nut. Cashews contain less fat than most other nuts, but the healthy fat that they do contain is essential for a properly functioning metabolism. Additionally, the American Heart Association states that monounsaturated fatty acids can help reduce "bad" cholesterol, and lower the risk for heart disease and stroke. This little delicious nut also contains 5 grams of protein.

INGREDIENTS

3.5 ounces (100 g) frozen, unsweetened acai puree

1 cup (30 g) fresh baby spinach

1 small frozen banana, peeled

½ avocado, halved, peeled and pitted

¼ cup (60 g) cashew butter

1½ cups (355 ml) unsweetened almond or cashew milk

1 teaspoon raw honey

4 ice cubes

TIP

Since you are only using a half of the avocado, keep the pit in the half not used to help keep it fresh and prevent some oxidative browning!

METHOD OF PREPARATION

Add the ingredients in the order listed to a high-powered blender. Puree until thick and creamy. Serve immediately.

Hormone-Balancing Blackberry, Acai, Maca, and Cacao Smoothie

SERVES 🥤🥤

This smoothie is great for hormone balancing. Maca, a cruciferous vegetable related to broccoli, cauliflower, cabbage, and kale, has long been used in Peru for culinary and medicinal purposes. It has traditionally been used to enhance fertility and sex drive, as well as to improve energy and stamina. A hormone-balancing superfood, maca contains eight essential amino acids, fatty acids, calcium, magnesium, iron, and potassium.

METHOD OF PREPARATION

Add the ingredients (except the cacao nibs and hazelnuts) in the order listed to a high-powered blender. Puree until thick and creamy. Garnish with the cacao nibs and hazelnuts, or additional blackberries with a few sprigs of mint and frozen yogurt. Serve immediately.

INGREDIENTS

7 ounces (200 g) frozen, unsweetened acai puree

1 cup (150 g) frozen organic blackberries

1 frozen banana, peeled

2 tablespoons (16 g) unsweetened cacao powder

1 tablespoon (8 g) maca powder

1 tablespoon (15 g) coconut butter

1 tablespoon (20 g) raw local honey

1½ cups (355 ml) unsweetened vanilla-flavored almond or cashew or coconut milk

Cacao nibs, for garnish

Chopped hazelnuts, for garnish

Pea Protein, Blueberry, Banana, and Acai Smoothie

SERVES 2

This smoothie contains a wonderful vegan source of protein made from yellow split peas. This protein source is great for those with whey or casein allergies. It is a rich source of plant-based iron; lysine, an essential amino acid that builds connective tissue like skin, cartilage, and bones; and magnesium, a mineral that plays a vital role in muscle movement and DNA repair. It is naturally free of gluten, cholesterol, and saturated fat and is a low-glycemic food. Phew! This protein-packed smoothie not only tastes great but will also keep you full all morning.

INGREDIENTS

3.5 ounces (100 g) frozen, unsweetened acai puree

2 cups (300 g) frozen organic blueberries

1 scoop vanilla-flavored pea protein powder

1 medium frozen banana, peeled

½ cup (120 ml) unsweetened vanilla-flavored almond or cashew or hemp milk

1½ cups (260 g) coconut yogurt

2 tablespoons (40 g) raw local honey

1 cup (150 g) ice cubes

TIP

If you happen to live in a place where blueberries are abundant in the summer months, freeze them on a sheet pan and then transfer to a freezer Ziploc. This is not only cheaper than buying frozen organic blueberries, but you are also freezing them at the peak of their nutritional value.

METHOD OF PREPARATION

Add the ingredients in the order listed to a high-powered blender. Puree until thick and creamy. Serve immediately.

Chocolate Acai Smoothie

SERVES

Cacao in a smoothie *and* it's a superfood?! Yes, please! Not only is unsweetened cacao a wonderful-tasting food, but it also contains some powerful benefits. It is known to decrease blood pressure and improve overall blood vessel health, and the consumption of this flavonoid-rich superfood has been shown to decrease LDL, or "bad," cholesterol and increase HDL, or "good," cholesterol.

INGREDIENTS

7 ounces (200 g) frozen, unsweetened acai puree

2 frozen bananas, peeled

2 tablespoons (16 g) unsweetened cacao powder

1 cup (235 ml) unsweetened almond or cashew milk

½ cup (75 g) frozen organic blueberries

1 tablespoon (20 g) raw local honey or agave

TIP

When replacing agave nectar for sugar in a recipe, use ⅔ cup (85 g) agave for every 1 cup (136 g) of sugar.

METHOD OF PREPARATION

Add the ingredients in the order listed to a high-powered blender. Puree until thick and creamy. Serve immediately.

Coconut Acai Smoothie

SERVES

This creamy smoothie is super hydrating. Coconut water, not to be mistaken with coconut milk, is free from fat and cholesterol and contains electrolytes, minerals like potassium and sodium. Maintaining a balance of electrolytes is essential for hydration, especially when sweating. Think of coconut water as nature's sports drink!

INGREDIENTS

7 ounces (200 g) frozen, unsweetened acai puree

2 medium frozen bananas, peeled

3 cups (705 ml) coconut water

1 cup (240 g) coconut yogurt

2 tablespoons (10 g) unsweetened coconut flakes, toasted

METHOD OF PREPARATION

Add the ingredients (except the coconut flakes) in the order listed to a high-powered blender. Puree until thick and creamy. Garnish with the toasted coconut and melted dark chocolate, if you wish, then serve immediately.

TRY THIS!

You can make your own coconut yogurt with two ingredients!

All you need is one 14-ounce (113 g) can of full-fat coconut milk + two capsules of vegan-friendly probiotic capsules.

Shake your coconut milk really well and pour into a clean, sterilized, dry, glass jar or bowl.

Empty your probiotic capsules into the yogurt and using a wooden or plastic spoon, stir well to incorporate.

Cover with cheesecloth and secure with a rubber band. Let the yogurt activate for 24 to 48 hours in a warm place.

Once it's as thick and tangy as you like, cover securely with a tight-fitting lid and refrigerate until cold. Store in fridge for up to 7 days.

Antinausea Ginger, Lime, and Acai Smoothie

SERVES 🥤🥤

This savory smoothie is excellent for relieving nausea. Whether for morning sickness, seasickness, or chemotherapy, this smoothie is a great way to naturally combat stomach upset. Ginger has also been shown to decrease exercise-induced muscle pain and soreness, lower blood sugar levels, improve heart disease risk factors, and help treat chronic indigestion.

INGREDIENTS

7 ounces (200 g) frozen, unsweetened acai puree

2 cups (310 g) frozen organic pineapple

2 cups (60 g) organic fresh baby spinach

2 cups (470 ml) unsweetened almond or cashew milk

1 cup (235 ml) coconut water

One 2-inch (5-cm) piece fresh ginger, peeled and roughly chopped

Juice of 1 lime

TIP

To peel ginger, hold the ginger root in one hand and a metal spoon in the other. Scrape the edge of the spoon along the peel of the ginger to peel off just the skin.

METHOD OF PREPARATION

Add the ingredients in the order listed to a high-powered blender. Puree until thick and creamy. Serve immediately.

Grapefruit, Acai, and Honey Smoothie

SERVES

This smoothie is a great immune booster. Fresh grapefruit juice is prized for its high content of vitamin C. This antioxidant has properties known to protect our cells from harmful bacteria and viruses. Raw local honey is a natural antibacterial and antifungal, soothes a sore throat, is great for digestive issues, and is packed with phytonutrients. The benefit of using local honey is that with just a spoonful a day, you can build your immunity through gradual exposure to local allergens, thereby reducing allergy symptoms.

INGREDIENTS

7 ounces (200 g) frozen, unsweetened acai puree

2 medium frozen bananas, peeled

1 cup (150 g) frozen organic blueberries

2 cups (470 ml) grapefruit juice

2 tablespoons (40 g) raw local honey

METHOD OF PREPARATION

Add the ingredients in the order listed to a high-powered blender. Puree until thick and creamy. Serve immediately.

Moringa Green Goddess Acai Smoothie

SERVES

Mmmmm . . . avocado, mango, spinach, moringa, almond butter, and raw honey! This smoothie is a powerhouse of vitamins, minerals, and antioxidants. Super rich in plant-based iron, this smoothie is great if you are feeling a little low on energy or have anemia.

METHOD OF PREPARATION

Add the ingredients in the order listed to a high-powered blender. Puree until thick and creamy. Serve immediately.

TIP

Add 1 teaspoon moringa powder to guacamole for a superfood-filled snack.

INGREDIENTS

3.5 ounces (100 g) frozen, unsweetened acai puree

1 frozen banana, peeled

1 ripe avocado, pitted, peeled, and chopped

½ cup (85 g) frozen organic mango chunks

1 cup (30 g) fresh organic baby spinach

1½ cups (355 ml) unsweetened almond or coconut milk

1 tablespoon (8 g) moringa powder

1 tablespoon (15 g) almond or peanut butter

1 tablespoon (20 g) raw local honey

Mangosteen, Mango, Banana, and Acai Smoothie

SERVES 2

Mangosteen and mango are high in vitamin C and fiber. Mangosteen is also a good source of magnesium and potassium. This immune-boosting, cancer-fighting superfood is a great one to add to your favorite smoothie!

TIP

Mangosteen powder can be mixed into yogurt for a quick snack.

INGREDIENTS

7 ounces (200 g) frozen, unsweetened acai puree

1 medium frozen banana, peeled

2 cups (340 g) frozen organic mango chunks

2 cups (470 ml) coconut water

1 tablespoon (8 g) mangosteen powder

1 tablespoon (20 g) raw local honey

METHOD OF PREPARATION

Add the ingredients in the order listed to a high-powered blender. Puree until thick and creamy. Serve immediately.

Matcha, Mint, and Acai Smoothie

SERVES 2

I love this combination of matcha, mint, and acai! It's so creamy and provides a natural boost of energy and a sense of focused calmness due to the amino acid L-theanine. The superfood matcha is full of catechins, more so than any other food that contains it. Catechins are antioxidants that have been shown to fight and possibly even prevent cancer.

TIP

Add 1 teaspoon of matcha powder to your morning oatmeal for an added energy and superfood boost.

INGREDIENTS

7 ounces (200 g) frozen, unsweetened acai puree

1 medium frozen banana, peeled

1 cup (235 ml) unsweetened almond or cashew milk

1 tablespoon (20 g) raw local honey

1 cup (30 g) organic baby spinach

¼ cup (12 g) organic fresh mint leaves

1 tablespoon (4 g) hulled hemp seeds

1 teaspoon matcha powder

METHOD OF PREPARATION

Add the ingredients in the order listed to a high-powered blender. Puree until thick and creamy. Serve immediately.

PB and J Acai Smoothie

SERVES **❚❚**

This smoothie might not have any extra superfood powers—besides the acai, that is—but who doesn't love PB and J? This one will take you back to childhood and in a truly delicious way.

INGREDIENTS

3.5 ounces (100 g) frozen, unsweetened acai puree

1 medium frozen banana, peeled

½ cup (120 g) smooth organic peanut butter

1 cup (150 g) frozen mixed organic berries

1 cup (235 ml) unsweetened almond, hemp, or cashew milk or 2% cow's milk

TIP

Read labels carefully. Many commercial brands of peanut butter have added sugar and hydrogenated oils.

METHOD OF PREPARATION

Add the ingredients in the order listed to a high-powered blender. Puree until thick and creamy. Serve immediately.

Pineapple, Acai, Coconut, and Cayenne Smoothie

SERVES

This smoothie is super interesting and some might even be a little reluctant to try it, but let me tell you why cayenne is such a superfood. Cayenne is rich in multiple vitamins and minerals, including vitamins C, B6, and E, potassium, manganese, and flavonoids, which have been shown to ease upset stomach, ulcers, sore throats, irritating coughs, and diarrhea, as well as being known as a digestive aid. Cayenne stimulates the digestive tract, increasing the flow of enzyme production and gastric juices, which in turn boosts metabolism and can help the body get rid of toxins. Combining cayenne with sweet pineapple, acai, and coconut gives this smoothie a delightful sweet kick!

INGREDIENTS

3.5 ounces (100 g) frozen, unsweetened acai puree

1 cup (150 g) frozen organic pineapple

1 frozen banana, peeled

2 cups (470 ml) coconut water

¼ to ½ teaspoon cayenne powder, to taste

TIP

If you cannot find frozen pineapple, cut up a ripe pineapple and place on a sheet pan. Place the sheet pan in the freezer. Once frozen, add to a Ziploc bag and freeze until needed.

METHOD OF PREPARATION

Add the ingredients in the order listed to a high-powered blender. Puree until thick and creamy. Serve immediately.

Protein
Pomegranate
Acai Smoothie

SERVES

Packed with protein, this smoothie helps reduce stress. Almonds are rich in tension-reducing vitamins and minerals like magnesium, zinc, vitamin E, and selenium. A deficiency in selenium has been associated with feelings of fatigue, depression, and anxiety.

INGREDIENTS

3.5 ounces (100 g) frozen, unsweetened acai puree

1 scoop vanilla-flavored protein powder, such as Vega One

1 cup (235 ml) unsweetened vanilla-flavored soy, hemp, cashew, or almond milk

½ cup (120 ml) pomegranate juice

½ frozen banana, peeled

1 tablespoon (15 g) almond butter

Pomegranate seeds, for garnish

TIP

Pomegranate juice is expensive. If you don't use all of it in your smoothies, try these fun uses: 1) add a little to fizzy water, 2) add it to your favorite vodka and soda beverage, or 3) freeze in ice cube trays and use it as festive ice cubes in a beverage—the options are endless!

METHOD OF PREPARATION

Add the ingredients (except the pomegranate seeds) in the order listed to a high-powered blender. Puree until thick and creamy. Garnish with the pomegranate seeds. Serve immediately.

Roasted Strawberry, Acai, Cardamom, and Balsamic Smoothie

SERVES

This dessert-like smoothie is not only exceptionally different, but it also contains cardamom. This spice is a great source of potassium, calcium, and magnesium. The volatile oils cardamom contains are what truly make this spice stand out. These oils include pinene, sabinene, myrcene, phellandrene, and limonene, all of which aid in digestion. Cardamom also contains potent antioxidants, making it a delicious superfood.

METHOD OF PREPARATION

1 Preheat the oven to 350°F (180°C, or gas mark 4) and line a baking sheet with parchment paper; set aside.

2 Wash and hull the strawberries, then cut them in half and place them in a medium bowl. Toss with 1 tablespoon (15 ml) of the maple syrup and 1 tablespoon (15 ml) of the balsamic vinegar. Toss until they are coated and transfer them to the prepared baking sheet.

3 Transfer to the middle rack and roast for 30 to 45 minutes, until nicely caramelized. Allow to cool.

4 Place the roasted strawberries, remaining 1 tablespoon (15 ml) maple syrup, remaining 1 teaspoon (5 ml) balsamic vinegar, acai, milk, yogurt, banana, cardamom, and ice to a high-powered blender. Puree until thick and creamy. Serve immediately.

INGREDIENTS

5 ounces (140 g) fresh organic strawberries

2 tablespoons (30 ml) pure maple syrup, divided

1 tablespoon (15 ml) plus 1 teaspoon (5 ml) balsamic vinegar, divided

3.5 ounces (100 g) frozen, unsweetened acai puree

1 cup (235 ml) non-fat cow's milk or plant milk of your choice

⅓ cup (80 g) Greek yogurt

1 frozen banana, peeled

½ teaspoon cardamom powder

1 cup (150 g) ice

Baobab, Strawberry, Banana, and Acai Smoothie

SERVES

This smoothie contains the superfood baobab, one of my favorite smoothie additions. Baobab is very high in vitamin C, making it an excellent collagen and elastin producer. Baobab also contains calcium, copper, iron, magnesium, and potassium, making it a great natural addition for those dealing with low iron or calcium deficiencies.

INGREDIENTS

3.5 ounces (100 g) frozen, unsweetened acai puree

1 frozen banana, peeled

2 cups (300 g) frozen organic strawberries

2 cups (470 ml) unsweetened vanilla-flavored almond or cashew milk

2 tablespoons (16 g) baobab powder

TIP

Add 2 tablespoons (16 g) baobab powder to your favorite gazpacho for an added superfood boost! I love it with watermelon and tomatoes.

METHOD OF PREPARATION

Add the ingredients in the order listed to a high-powered blender. Puree until thick and creamy. Serve immediately.

Watermelon, Acai, and Baobab Smoothie

SERVES

This is a favorite summertime smoothie. Super light and fruity, it packs a trio of superfoods. Acai, chia seeds, and baobab make this smoothie an ultimate powerhouse of vitamins, minerals, and antioxidants! Add in some sweet summertime watermelon and in jumps another incredible antioxidant, lycopene.

INGREDIENTS

7 ounces (200 g) frozen, unsweetened acai puree

4 cups (600 g) cubed watermelon

3 tablespoons (21 g) chia seeds

2 tablespoons (16 g) baobab powder

1 teaspoon lemon zest

METHOD OF PREPARATION

Add the ingredients in the order listed to a high-powered blender. Puree until thick and creamy. Serve immediately.

PART II

Smoothie Bowls

Acai, Berry, and Mango Layered Smoothie Bowl

SERVES 👥

This smoothie bowl is just gorgeous to look at, with a swirl of magenta acai and orange mango. If you don't want to worry about the double-colored bowl, you can always add all the ingredients to the blender at once—it will still taste just as delectable!

METHOD OF PREPARATION

1 Run the acai packet under warm water for 10 seconds.

2 In a high-powered blender, add the acai, frozen mixed berries, and milk. Blend until smooth and transfer to a pitcher until ready to serve.

3 Rinse the blender jar and add the frozen mango, banana, and coconut water. Blend until smooth. Add half of each smoothie to each of two bowls, layering them as desired.

4 Top with your desired toppings. Serve immediately.

INGREDIENTS

3.5 ounces (100 g) frozen, unsweetened acai puree

½ cup (75 g) frozen organic mixed berries

¾ cup (180 ml) unsweetened almond, flax, or cashew milk

1 cup (170 g) organic frozen mango

½ frozen banana, peeled

¾ cup (180 ml) coconut water

Optional Toppings

½ cup (75 g) fresh organic blueberries

½ cup (75 g) fresh organic raspberries or blackberries

½ cup (40 g) unsweetened coconut flakes

½ cup (80 g) granola

Sprinkle of chia seeds

Acai and Oatmeal Cookie Smoothie Bowl

SERVES 💡💡

An oatmeal cookie smoothie bowl? Yes, please! Not only does this smoothie bowl taste great, but it also contains oats. Oats are rich in B vitamins, magnesium, and fiber, all of which are vital nutrients for reducing stress. Oats are also one of the best food sources for the production of serotonin, the antidepressant hormone.

METHOD OF PREPARATION

1 Run the acai packet under warm water for 10 seconds.

2 In a high-powered blender, add the acai, banana, oats, dates, cacao nibs, coconut, almond butter, and milk. Puree until smooth. Divide between two bowls.

3 Top with your desired toppings. Serve immediately.

INGREDIENTS

3.5 ounces (100 g) frozen, unsweetened acai puree

1 frozen banana, peeled

¼ cup (20 g) old-fashioned oats

4 Medjool dates, pitted

2 tablespoons (18 g) cacao nibs

2 tablespoons (10 g) unsweetened coconut flakes

2 tablespoons (30 g) almond butter

¾ cup (180 ml) almond milk

Optional Toppings

2 tablespoons (10 g) old-fashioned oats

2 tablespoons (18 g) cacao nibs

Fresh blueberries

Fresh raspberries

Acai, Turmeric, and Pumpkin Spice Smoothie Bowl

SERVES 🥣🥣

This smoothie bowl is a little bit of autumn comfort. It also contains two powerful spices: turmeric and nutmeg. Turmeric is that amazing anti-inflammation spice that contains curcumin, which aids in digestion, fights cancer, eases arthritis, and lowers the risk of heart attack. Nutmeg contains fiber, manganese, thiamin, vitamin B6, folate, magnesium, and copper. It has been shown to relieve pain, soothe indigestion, and strengthen cognitive function. That's quite a lot of power in one little smoothie bowl!

METHOD OF PREPARATION

1 Run the acai packet under warm water for 10 seconds.

2 In a high-powered blender, add the acai, banana, pumpkin, apple, almond butter, cinnamon, turmeric, nutmeg, and milk. Puree until smooth. Divide between two bowls.

3 Top with your desired toppings. Serve immediately.

INGREDIENTS

7 ounces (200 g) frozen, unsweetened acai puree

1 frozen banana, peeled

⅔ cup (180 g) 100% pumpkin puree

1 cup (150 g) chopped red apple

2 tablespoons (30 g) almond butter

1 teaspoon ground cinnamon

1 teaspoon ground turmeric

¼ teaspoon ground nutmeg

½ cup (120 ml) unsweetened vanilla-flavored almond or cashew milk

Optional Toppings

2 tablespoons (14 g) pumpkin seeds

2 tablespoons (14 g) pomegranate arils

Sliced banana

Acai, Dark Chocolate, Maca, and Blackberry Smoothie Bowl

SERVES 2

This smoothie bowl is best used for hormone balancing. Maca, a Peruvian cruciferous vegetable, is known for increasing libido, boosting energy and endurance, increasing fertility, and reducing menopause symptoms. Maca powder has been shown to balance levels of the hormone estrogen. Some studies have shown that adding maca to your daily routine reduces menopausal symptoms such as hot flashes and night sweats.

METHOD OF PREPARATION

1 Run the acai packet under warm water for 10 seconds.

2 In a high-powered blender, add the acai, banana, blackberries, protein powder, cacao, maca, and milk. Blend until smooth. Divide between two bowls.

3 Top with your desired toppings. Serve immediately.

INGREDIENTS

3.5 ounces (100 g) frozen, unsweetened acai puree

1 frozen banana, peeled

1 cup (150 g) frozen organic blackberries

2 scoops chocolate-flavored plant-based protein powder

1 tablespoon (8 g) unsweetened cacao powder

1 tablespoon (8 g) maca powder

1 to 1½ cups (235 to 355 ml) non-fat milk or plant milk of your choice

Optional Toppings

1 cup (150 g) fresh organic mixed berries

2 tablespoons (18 g) cacao nibs

Sprinkle of coconut flakes or granola

Acai, Blueberry, Mango, Mangosteen, and Spirulina Smoothie Bowl

SERVES 👥

This smoothie bowl is a nutritional powerhouse of superfoods: acai, blueberries, mangosteen, and spirulina all in one bowl. Let's focus on spirulina for this one. This alga is considered one of the most nutritionally complete foods out there. Spirulina is one of the richest sources of beta-carotene, plus it's a complete protein and contains all essential amino acids. It also contains an abundance of fatty acids, one of which is super rare, gamma linolenic acid. This superfood is great at fighting allergy symptoms and boosting the immune system with vitamins A, B, C, E, and K as well as minerals potassium, calcium, chromium, copper, iron, and magnesium. That is quite a superfood!

METHOD OF PREPARATION

1 Run the acai packet under warm water for 10 seconds.

2 In a high-powered blender, add the acai, banana, blueberries, mango, protein powder, spirulina, mangosteen powder, and milk. Puree until smooth. Divide between two bowls.

3 Top with your desired toppings. Serve immediately.

INGREDIENTS

3.5 ounces (100 g) frozen, unsweetened acai puree

1 frozen banana, peeled

1 cup (150 g) frozen organic wild blueberries

½ cup (85 g) frozen organic mango

2 scoops vanilla-flavored plant-based protein powder

2 teaspoons spirulina powder

2 teaspoons mangosteen powder

1½ cups (355 ml) unsweetened almond or flax milk

Optional Toppings

1 cup (150 g) organic fresh fruit, such as blueberries, raspberries, blackberries, and/or chopped dragon fruit

1 banana, sliced

2 tablespoons (18 g) sunflower seeds and/or (14 g) chia seeds

Sprinkle of granola

Acai, Cherry, and Dark Chocolate Protein Smoothie Bowl

SERVES 2

This smoothie bowl tastes like delectable chocolate-covered cherries! Not only that, but the addition of raw, unsweetened cacao powder has been shown to help lower "bad" cholesterol, blood pressure, and the risk of cardiovascular disease. Besides being a great anti-inflammatory, cacao is a natural stimulant, due to its caffeine content, so it gives a little burst of energy.

METHOD OF PREPARATION

1 Run the acai packet under warm water for 10 seconds.

2 In a high-powered blender, add the acai, banana, cherries, protein powder, cacao powder, and milk. Blend until smooth. Divide between two bowls.

3 Top with your desired toppings. Serve immediately.

INGREDIENTS

3.5 ounces (100 g) frozen, unsweetened acai puree

1 frozen banana, peeled

1 cup (150 g) frozen organic pitted sweet cherries

2 scoops chocolate-flavored plant-based protein powder

¼ cup (30 g) unsweetened dark cacao powder

1 cup (235 ml) unsweetened vanilla-flavored almond, cashew, or hemp milk

Optional Toppings

2 cups (300 g) fresh organic cherries

¼ cup (36 g) cacao nibs

¼ cup (35 g) raw almonds

¼ cup (20 g) unsweetened coconut flakes

Acai, Cream of Coconut, and Blue Spirulina Smoothie Bowl

SERVES 2

This light purplish-blue smoothie bowl is just gorgeous, plus it contains one of the most nutritious superfoods out there. Blue spirulina, related to its green algae counterpart, looks like its name and is bright blue in color. This powerful algae has been shown to bind with heavy metals and toxins in the body and help remove them. It is high in protein, may help with weight loss, boosts energy levels, and aids the digestive process.

TIP

Spirulina contains oxygen sensitive nutrients that can diminish after opening. Store your opened bag in the refrigerator and make sure to use it up within a few months after opening.

INGREDIENTS

3.5 ounces (100 g) frozen, unsweetened acai puree

2 frozen bananas, peeled

½ cup (75 g) green grapes, frozen

2 teaspoons spirulina powder

1 can (5.4 ounces; 153 g) cream of coconut

Optional Toppings

½ cup (75 g) frozen organic blackberries

½ cup (75 g) frozen organic blueberries

½ cup (75 g) chopped dragon fruit

METHOD OF PREPARATION

1 Run the acai packet under warm water for 10 seconds.

2 In a high-powered blender, add the acai, banana, grapes, spirulina, and cream of coconut. Blend until smooth. Divide between two bowls.

3 Top with your desired toppings. Serve immediately.

Acai, Dark Chocolate, and Strawberry Smoothie Bowl

SERVES ●●

A chocolate-covered strawberry, that's what this smoothie bowl brings to mind. Full of protein, vitamins, minerals, and antioxidants, this bowl is an indulgent way to start or end the day.

METHOD OF PREPARATION

1 Run the acai packet under warm water for 10 seconds.

2 In a high-powered blender, add the acai, strawberries, protein powder, cacao powder, and milk. Blend until smooth. Divide between two bowls.

3 Top with your desired toppings. Serve immediately.

INGREDIENTS

7 ounces (200 g) frozen, unsweetened acai puree

2 cups (300 g) frozen organic strawberries

2 scoops chocolate-flavored plant-based protein powder

1 tablespoon (8 g) unsweetened dark cacao powder

1 cup (235 ml) unsweetened chocolate-flavored almond milk

Optional Toppings

1 cup (170 g) hulled and sliced fresh organic strawberries

½ cup (80 g) chocolate granola

2 tablespoons (10 g) unsweetened coconut flakes

Acai, Mint, Lime, Papaya, and Kiwi Smoothie Bowl

SERVES 🍒🍒

This tropical smoothie bowl is so beautiful as well as delightfully refreshing. The combination of acai, mint, lime, papaya, and kiwi makes it a great source of vitamin C and fiber!

METHOD OF PREPARATION

1 Run the acai packet under warm water for 10 seconds.

2 In a high-powered blender, add the acai, banana, papaya, kiwi, mint, lime juice, and almond milk. Blend until smooth. Divide between two bowls, or serve in the halves of a papaya.

3 Top with your desired toppings. Serve immediately.

INGREDIENTS

7 ounces (200 g) frozen, unsweetened acai puree

1 frozen banana, peeled

1 cup (150 g) frozen papaya chunks

2 kiwi, peeled and previously frozen

¼ cup (8 g) fresh mint leaves

¼ cup (60 ml) fresh lime juice

1 cup (235 ml) unsweetened almond milk

Optional Toppings

1 papaya, cut in half lengthwise, seeds removed, and flesh scooped out

½ cup (75 g) frozen organic mixed berries

2 tablespoons (18 g) chopped nuts

1 kiwi, peeled and sliced

Berry Coconut Blast Smoothie Bowl

SERVES

This smoothie bowl is simple and delicious. Filled with berries, this bowl is low in calories and sugar and high in fiber, vitamin C, folate, and potassium. This go-to smoothie bowl will always hit the spot.

METHOD OF PREPARATION

1 Run the acai packet under warm water for 10 seconds.

2 In a high-powered blender, add the acai, banana, berries, and coconut water. Blend until smooth. Divide between two bowls.

3 Top with your desired toppings. Serve immediately.

INGREDIENTS

7 ounces (200 g) frozen, unsweetened acai puree

1 frozen banana, peeled

1 cup (150 g) frozen organic mixed berries

1 cup (235 ml) coconut water

Optional Toppings

½ cup (75 g) fresh organic blueberries

½ cup (75 g) fresh organic raspberries or blackberries

½ cup (40 g) unsweetened coconut flakes

½ cup (80 g) granola

Fig, Acai, and Blueberry Smoothie Bowl

SERVES 🍒🍒

If you are lucky enough to have a fig tree, you know that they all ripen at the same time! I am always on the lookout for ways to use them up when they come to that sweet milky ripeness. This smoothie bowl utilizes fresh figs at their peak. The fig is a natural laxative because of its high fiber content, is a prebiotic that helps support the preexisting good bacteria in the gut, and is a good source of calcium and potassium.

METHOD OF PREPARATION

1 Run the acai packet under warm water for 10 seconds.

2 In a high-powered blender, add the acai, blueberries, spinach, figs, yogurt, and milk. Blend until smooth and creamy. Divide between two bowls.

3 Top with your desired toppings. Serve immediately.

INGREDIENTS

7 ounces (200 g) frozen, unsweetened acai puree

1½ cups (225 g) frozen organic blueberries

1½ cups (45 g) fresh organic baby spinach

4 fresh organic figs, stemmed and previously frozen

½ cup (120 g) non-fat Greek yogurt

¼ to ½ cup (60 to 120 ml) non-fat milk

Optional Toppings

4 fresh ripe figs, stemmed and sliced

½ cup (75 g) fresh organic raspberries and/or blueberries

½ cup (80 g) granola

Peaches and Cream Acai Smoothie Bowl with Granola Crumble

SERVES 🍒🍒

This smoothie bowl, reminiscent of a peach crumble, is best made when peaches are at their peak in summer. Adding the cinnamon sets it over the top nutritionally. This spice is extremely high in antioxidants, is a potent anti-inflammatory, and has been shown with daily consumption to treat chronic issues like arthritis and autoimmune diseases.

TIP

Nectarines and plums are great alternatives to the peaches in this recipe.

INGREDIENTS

3.5 ounces (100 g) frozen, unsweetened acai puree

2 cups (300 g) frozen organic peach slices

1 tablespoon (15 ml) maple syrup

1 teaspoon vanilla extract

½ teaspoon ground cinnamon

¾ cup (180 ml) full-fat canned coconut milk

Optional Toppings

1½ cups (240 g) sliced organic peaches

1 cup (160 g) almond granola

METHOD OF PREPARATION

1 Run the acai packet under warm water for 10 seconds.

2 In a high-powered blender, add the acai, peaches, maple syrup, vanilla, cinnamon, and coconut milk. Blend until smooth. Divide between two bowls.

3 Top with your desired toppings. Serve immediately.

Acai, Mango, and Pineapple Smoothie Bowl

SERVES 2

This is another delightful tropical smoothie bowl filled with some nutritional powerhouses: mango, acai, and mangosteen. We've talked about mangosteen's vitamin, mineral, and antioxidant content, but one thing I haven't discussed is mangosteen's use in treating Alzheimer's disease, fighting acne, repairing cells, fighting cancer, and lowering blood pressure. This little fruit has been part of traditional medicine in various Asian countries for a long time and is finally getting the attention it deserves elsewhere, too.

METHOD OF PREPARATION

1 Run the acai packet under warm water for 10 seconds.

2 In a high-powered blender, add the acai, mango, pineapple, mangosteen powder, and coconut milk. Blend until smooth. Divide between two bowls.

3 Top with your desired toppings. Serve immediately.

INGREDIENTS

3.5 ounces (100 g) frozen, unsweetened acai puree

1 cup (170 g) frozen organic mango chunks

1 cup (150 g) frozen organic pineapple chunks

2 teaspoons mangosteen powder

1 cup (235 ml) coconut milk

Optional Toppings

½ cup (85 g) sliced mango

½ cup (85 g) halved strawberries

¼ cup (36 g) pomegranate arils

¼ cup (20 g) unsweetened shredded coconut

Fresh mint

Blackberry, Rosewater, and Acai Smoothie Bowl

SERVES

Wow, this smoothie bowl is simply otherworldly! The addition of rosewater may seem strange, but there are so many health benefits. Rosewater is a strong anti-inflammatory, treating both internal and external ailments such as eczema and rosacea. It is also a powerful antiseptic, used to treat and prevent infections. Plus it contains powerful antioxidants, which protect cells from damage, and has been shown to positively influence digestion and relieve stomach upset.

METHOD OF PREPARATION

1 Run the acai packet under warm water for 10 seconds.

2 In a high-powered blender, add the acai, banana, blackberries, flax meal, rosewater, and almond milk. Blend until smooth. Divide between two bowls.

3 Top with your desired toppings. Serve immediately.

INGREDIENTS

3.5 ounces (100 g) frozen, unsweetened acai puree

1 frozen banana, peeled

1½ cups (225 g) frozen organic blackberries

2 tablespoons (16 g) flaxseed meal

2 teaspoons rosewater

½ to ¾ cup (120 to 180 ml) unsweetened almond milk

Optional Toppings

½ cup (75 g) frozen organic blackberries

¼ cup (38 g) frozen mixed berries

¼ cup (35 g) dried mulberries

Sprinkle of flaxseed

Cantaloupe, Acai, and Goji Berry Smoothie Bowl

SERVES 🍒🍒

This smoothie is best made when cantaloupe is at its summer's peak. Buy a couple of extra super sweet melons, then peel, chop, and freeze them for this bowl—you won't be sorry for the little bit of extra work. The other awesome superfood included in this smoothie bowl is the goji berry. This berry offers a good serving of fiber, protein, and essential amino acids, making it a very unique fruit. Goji berries are also high in vitamin A, vitamin C, and iron. This powerful antioxidant is a great inflammation fighter as well.

INGREDIENTS

7 ounces (200 g) frozen, unsweetened acai puree

2 cups (320 g) chopped cantaloupe, frozen

1 teaspoon flaxseed meal

½ to ¾ cup (120 to 180 ml) unsweetened almond or cashew milk

Optional Toppings

¼ cup (36 g) goji berries

1 tablespoon (9 g) hemp hearts

Fresh cantaloupe balls

Fresh sliced strawberries

Unsweetened coconut flakes

METHOD OF PREPARATION

1 Run the acai packet under warm water for 10 seconds.

2 In a high-powered blender, add the acai, cantaloupe, flax meal, and milk. Blend until smooth. Divide between two bowls.

3 Top with your desired toppings. Serve immediately.

Chocolate, Chia, Raspberry, and Acai Smoothie Bowl

SERVES 2

This custard-like smoothie bowl is full of superfoods! Dark raw cacao, chia seeds, and acai make this bowl an over-the-top nutritional powerhouse. I love this for breakfast, lunch, a snack, or dessert; it's so versatile.

METHOD OF PREPARATION

1 Run the acai packet under warm water for 10 seconds.

2 In a high-powered blender, add the acai, raspberries, cacao, chia seeds, and milk. Blend until smooth. Divide between two bowls.

3 Top with your desired toppings. Serve immediately.

TIP

To make a smoothie bowl ahead of time, make it and freeze it in a glass mason jar. Allow it to defrost in the fridge overnight and voila! You have an instant breakfast.

INGREDIENTS

3.5 ounces (100 g) frozen, unsweetened acai puree

1½ cups (225 g) frozen organic raspberries

1 tablespoon (8 g) unsweetened cacao powder

1 tablespoon (7 g) chia seeds

¾ cup (180 ml) unsweetened almond milk or milk of your choice

Optional Toppings

1 cup (150 g) organic raspberries

1 tablespoon (7 g) chia seeds

1 tablespoon (9 g) cacao nibs

Clean Green Acai Spirulina Smoothie Bowl

SERVES

INGREDIENTS

7 ounces (200 g) frozen, unsweetened acai puree

2 cups (130 g) fresh organic baby kale

1 cup (30 g) fresh organic baby spinach

2 frozen bananas, peeled

½ teaspoon spirulina powder

1 cup (235 ml) unsweetened almond or coconut milk

Optional Toppings

1 banana, sliced

¼ cup (35 g) raw almonds

½ cup (75 g) fresh organic berries

¼ cup (36 g) raw pumpkin seeds

¼ cup (20 g) unsweetened flaked coconut

This smoothie bowl is quite unique: with a whopping 3 cups (160 g) of greens plus spirulina, it is a superfood overload! High in fiber, plant-based iron, magnesium, potassium, calcium, and folate, this bowl is a perfect start to your day.

METHOD OF PREPARATION

1 Run the acai packet under warm water for 10 seconds.

2 In a high-powered blender, add the acai, kale, spinach, bananas, spirulina, and almond milk. Blend until smooth and creamy. Divide between two bowls.

3 Top with your desired toppings. Serve immediately.

TIP

Buying washed baby spinach and kale makes this smoothie bowl a snap to put together on a busy morning!

Dragon Fruit, Acai, Baobab, and Coconut Yogurt Smoothie Bowl

SERVES 2

Dragon fruit is the star of this smoothie bowl. Known for its vibrant red skin and sweet, seed-speckled pulp, this unique superfood is packed with essential vitamins and minerals. Antioxidant-rich dragon fruit has been shown to neutralize free radicals, preventing chronic disease, cell damage, and inflammation.

METHOD OF PREPARATION

1 Run the acai packet under warm water for 10 seconds.

2 In a high-powered blender, add the acai, dragon fruit, bananas, protein powder, baobab powder, and cashew milk. Blend until smooth and creamy. Divide between two bowls.

3 Top with your desired toppings. Serve immediately.

INGREDIENTS

7 ounces (200 g) frozen, unsweetened acai puree

1 packet (100 g) frozen, unsweetened dragon fruit (such as Pitaya Plus brand)

2 frozen bananas, peeled

¼ cup (59 g) vanilla-flavored vegan protein powder (such as Vega One or Nuzest brand)

1 scoop baobab powder (such as Kaibae brand)

½ to ¾ cup (120 to 180 ml) unsweetened cashew or almond milk

Optional Toppings

½ cup (120 g) coconut yogurt

½ cup (75 g) chopped red or white dragon fruit

½ cup (80 g) granola

Green Grape, Kiwi, and Acai Smoothie Bowl with Spirulina

SERVES

INGREDIENTS

3.5 ounces (100 g) frozen, unsweetened acai puree

2 frozen bananas, peeled

1 cup (150 g) green grapes

1 cup (30 g) fresh organic baby spinach

1 teaspoon blue spirulina powder

½ avocado, peeled and pitted

1 cup (235 ml) unsweetened almond or cashew milk

Optional Toppings

1 cup (150 g) green grapes, sliced

1 tablespoon (7 g) chia seeds

¼ cup (38 g) peeled, chopped kiwi

Sprinkle of whole oats

You may have noticed that this isn't the first smoothie bowl to use spirulina, and that's because it truly is an incredible superfood! I actually include it in all of my smoothies and smoothie bowls, because that's how much I love its benefits. Its powerful antioxidant and anti-inflammatory properties alone are a great reason to add it to your daily routine.

METHOD OF PREPARATION

1 Run the acai packet under warm water for 10 seconds.

2 In a high-powered blender, add the acai, bananas, grapes, spinach, spirulina, avocado, and almond milk. Blend until smooth. Divide between two bowls.

3 Top with your desired toppings. Serve immediately.

Peanut Butter and Jelly
Acai Smoothie Bowl with Hemp Seeds

SERVES 🍴🍴

Hemp seeds are one the best plant-based sources of protein around. They are a complete source of protein, providing all nine essential amino acids. In addition, hemp seeds are full of essential fatty acids, which promote healthy skin and hair and lower inflammation in the body.

METHOD OF PREPARATION

1 Run the acai packet under warm water for 10 seconds.

2 In a high-powered blender, add the acai, banana, peanut butter powder, milk, spinach, and berries. Blend until smooth and thick. Divide between two bowls.

3 Top with your desired toppings. Serve immediately.

INGREDIENTS

7 ounces (200 g) frozen, unsweetened acai puree

1 frozen banana, peeled

3 tablespoons (24 g) peanut butter powder

½ to ¾ cup (120 to 180 ml) unsweetened coconut, almond, or cashew milk

1 cup (30 g) fresh organic baby spinach

¼ cup (38 g) mixed frozen organic berries

Optional Toppings

1 banana, peeled and sliced

2 tablespoons (10 g) unsweetened shredded coconut

2 tablespoons (18 g) hulled hemp seeds

TIP
Hulled hemp seeds go rancid very quickly. To extend their shelf life, store in a glass jar with a tight-fitting lid in the freezer. This will extend their shelf life to about a year.

Probiotic Acai, Mango, and Turmeric Smoothie Bowl

SERVES 2

I am a huge fan of the pre- and probiotic to ensure a healthy digestive tract! Pre- and probiotics need each other to work properly. The mango, because of its nondigestible fiber content, is a good prebiotic. Kefir, a good probiotic, helps balance the friendly bacteria in your digestive tract, and helps prevent and treat diarrhea. These incredible probiotics have also been shown to reduce the severity of certain allergies and eczema. A plant-based kefir is now available as well!

INGREDIENTS

3.5 ounces (100 g) frozen, unsweetened acai puree

1 cup (170 g) frozen organic mango chunks

1 seedless navel orange, peeled

2 teaspoons turmeric powder

1 teaspoon chia seeds

1½ cups (355 ml) kefir

Optional Toppings

½ cup (75 g) sliced organic peach or nectarine

½ cup (75 g) frozen mixed berries

½ cup (80 g) granola

1 teaspoon chia seeds

2 tablespoons (30 ml) kefir

METHOD OF PREPARATION

1 Run the acai packet under warm water for 10 seconds.

2 In a high-powered blender, add the acai, mango, orange, turmeric, chia seeds, and kefir. Blend until smooth.

3 Top with your desired toppings. Serve immediately.

Protein, Macadamia Nut, Blueberry, Maca, and Acai Smoothie Bowl

SERVES

Macadamia nut milk, one of the new "milks" out on the market now, is super creamy and loaded with micronutrients, offering lots of vitamins and minerals in one serving. It's a good source of fiber, has lots of healthy monounsaturated fatty acids, and contains vitamin B6, calcium, copper, iron, magnesium, manganese, potassium, selenium, and zinc. This nut has also been shown to help lower cholesterol and blood pressure, and the antioxidants it contains are a great rejuvenator for skin and hair.

INGREDIENTS

7 ounces (200 g) frozen, unsweetened acai puree

1 frozen banana, peeled

1 cup (150 g) frozen organic wild blueberries

2 scoops vanilla-flavored plant-based protein powder

2 tablespoons (16 g) maca powder

¾ cup (180 ml) macadamia nut milk

Optional Toppings

1 cup (150 g) frozen organic wild blueberries

¼ cup (35 g) chopped macadamia nuts

Sprinkle of chia seeds

TIP

Macadamia nut milk is incredibly thick and creamy. Use it to make a matcha or regular latte and you will not be disappointed; its texture is like whole milk!

METHOD OF PREPARATION

1 Run the acai packet under warm water for 10 seconds.

2 In a high-powered blender, add the acai, banana, blueberries, protein powder, maca, and nut milk. Blend until smooth. Divide between two bowls.

3 Top with your desired toppings. Serve immediately.

Rainbow Spirulina Acai Bowl with Butterfly Pea Flower

INGREDIENTS

7 ounces (200 g) frozen, unsweetened acai puree, divided

2 frozen bananas, peeled, divided

2 tablespoons (16 g) hulled hemp seeds, divided

2 tablespoons (14 g) chia seeds, divided

½ cup (120 ml) coconut milk, divided

1 teaspoon blue spirulina powder

1 teaspoon butterfly pea powder

Optional Toppings

½ cup (75 g) chopped dragon fruit

½ cup (75 g) frozen blackberries

¼ cup (38 g) peeled, chopped kiwi

¼ cup (36 g) crushed goji berries

The lesser-known ingredient in this smoothie bowl is butterfly pea flower tea. It is similar to green tea in its potent levels of antioxidants. Studied for its protection against skin and premature aging, it has also been shown to help fight inflammation in the body.

METHOD OF PREPARATION

1 Run the acai packet under warm water for 10 seconds.

2 In a high-powered blender, add 3.5 ounces (100 g) of the acai, 1 of the bananas, 1 tablespoon (8 g) of the hemp seeds, 1 tablespoon (7 g) of the chia seeds, ¼ cup (60 ml) of the coconut milk, and the spirulina. Blend until smooth. Divide between two bowls and rinse your blender jar.

3 In the blender, add 3.5 ounces (100 g) acai, remaining 1 banana, remaining 1 tablespoon (8 g) hemp seeds, remaining 1 tablespoon (7 g) chia seeds, remaining ¼ cup (60 ml) coconut milk, and the butterfly pea powder. Blend until smooth. Divide between the two bowls and swirl with the blue smoothie.

4 Top with your desired toppings. Serve immediately.

PART III

Sweet Treats

Acai, Chia Pudding, Berry, and Granola Overnight Parfait

SERVES 2

Don't let the "overnight" in the title fool you: this parfait is so simple and easy to grab on a busy day! It will keep you full all morning as well as start the day with a punch of vitamins, minerals, and antioxidants. Feel free to switch up the milks used as well as add a twist with your favorite nut butter and berries.

METHOD OF PREPARATION

1 In a medium bowl, whisk together the chia seeds, 1 cup (235 ml) of the cashew milk, and the vanilla. Allow to sit for 30 minutes, or until the seeds have absorbed all the liquid; whisk halfway through.

2 Meanwhile, in a high-powered blender, add the acai powder, berries, banana, almond butter, coconut, and remaining ¼ cup (60 ml) cashew milk. Blend until smooth.

3 To assemble the parfaits, add half of the chia mixture to the bottom of a glass, add half of the granola, and then top with half of the acai smoothie and half of the berries. Repeat for the other parfait.

4 Cover and transfer to the fridge and refrigerate overnight.

INGREDIENTS

¼ cup (28 g) chia seeds

1¼ cups (295 ml) unsweetened cashew milk, divided

1 teaspoon vanilla extract

1 tablespoon (8 g) acai powder

1 cup (150 g) fresh organic berries, such as strawberries, raspberries, and/or blueberries

1 ripe banana, peeled

1 tablespoon (15 g) almond butter

2 tablespoons (10 g) unsweetened shredded coconut

Toppings

½ cup (80 g) granola

½ cup (75 g) fresh organic berries, such as blueberries and raspberries

Acai Dark Cacao Brownies

MAKES 12 BROWNIES

You can feel great about indulging in these super fudgy brownies with your family. Loaded with oats, acai, raw cacao, protein powder, pumpkin, and maple syrup, they should be called superfood brownies! The crunch you get from the cacao nibs is just an extra delightful bonus.

INGREDIENTS

2 cups (240 g) ground oat flour

½ cup (60 g) acai powder

½ cup (60 g) raw cacao powder

¼ cup (30 g) vanilla-flavored plant-based protein powder

⅔ teaspoon baking soda

Pinch of salt

2 cups (480 g) canned 100% organic pumpkin puree

⅔ cup (160 ml) maple syrup

2 tablespoons (30 ml) fresh squeezed lemon juice

½ cup (65 g) cacao nibs

METHOD OF PREPARATION

1 Preheat the oven to 350°F (180°C, or gas mark 4). Grease an 8 x 8-inch (20 x 20-cm) nonstick brownie pan and line it with parchment paper; set aside.

2 In a large bowl, whisk together the oat flour, acai powder, raw cacao powder, protein powder, baking soda, and salt. In a separate medium bowl, whisk together the pumpkin puree, maple syrup, and lemon juice.

3 Add the wet ingredients to the dry ingredients and blend with a wooden spoon until just combined. Stir in the cacao nibs.

4 Spread into the prepared baking pan and transfer to the oven. Bake for 45 to 50 minutes or until a toothpick inserted in the center comes out with few crumbs—more for fudgier brownies, less for drier brownies.

5 Remove from the oven and cool before cutting into 12 rectangles.

TIP

Brownies are great straight out of the freezer. If there are any leftovers, store the extras in an airtight container for a frozen treat!

Acai, Banana, and Chai Pancakes

INGREDIENTS

2 cups (240 g) almond meal

¾ cup (60 g) unsweetened shredded coconut

¼ cup (30 g) acai powder

½ teaspoon salt

2 teaspoons ground cinnamon

¼ teaspoon ground turmeric

¼ teaspoon ground cloves

¼ teaspoon ground cardamom

¼ teaspoon ground ginger

6 large eggs

½ cup (120 ml) unsweetened almond or coconut milk

2 tablespoons (30 ml) maple syrup

4 tablespoons (60 g) coconut oil, divided

3 bananas, peeled and sliced

Optional Toppings

½ cup (75 g) chopped walnuts, pecans, or almonds

½ cup (40 g) unsweetened shredded coconut

2 bananas, sliced

Maple syrup

These pancakes scream "autumn" and are such a delightful warming treat. You can easily make these all plant-based by switching out the eggs for aquafaba. Aquafaba is the starchy liquid you typically drain and throw away from a can of chickpeas. To measure and substitute for the amount of eggs needed, simply shake a can of unopened chickpeas vigorously. Drain the chickpeas through a fine-mesh strainer over a bowl (reserve the chickpeas for later use) and then whisk the aquafaba to measure. One whole egg is equal to 3 tablespoons (45 ml) of frothy aquafaba.

METHOD OF PREPARATION

1 In a large bowl, whisk together the almond meal, coconut, acai powder, salt, and spices.

2 In a separate large bowl, whisk together the eggs, milk, and maple syrup. Stir the wet ingredients into the dry until just incorporated; do not overmix.

3 Melt 1 tablespoon (15 g) of the coconut oil in a large nonstick sauté pan or griddle pan over medium heat. Once hot, reduce the heat to medium-low and add heaping tablespoons (15 g) of the pancake mixture. Add banana slices to each uncooked side of the pancake.

4 Once the pancakes have cooked on the first side for about 5 minutes and are golden, very carefully flip over to the other side. Cook an additional 3 to 5 minutes on the second side. Keep the cooked pancakes warm and continue with the remaining batter, coconut oil, and bananas.

5 Top with your desired toppings and serve immediately.

Acai, Cacao, and Walnut Energy Bites

MAKES 20 BITES

Energy bites are all the rage in my house, kind of like a magical raw cookie dough with tons of health benefits! These little chocolate-almond-date bites are a great energy source during a long run or other intense workout, or even as an after-school snack.

INGREDIENTS

1 cup (180 g) pitted and packed Medjool dates

2 cups (300 g) raw walnuts

6 tablespoons (48 g) unsweetened cacao powder

2 tablespoons (18 g) hemp seeds

1 tablespoon (8 g) acai powder

½ teaspoon pink Himalayan sea salt

3 tablespoons (45 g) creamy almond or peanut butter

1 tablespoon (15 g) coconut oil, melted

For Rolling

2 tablespoons (10 g) unsweetened shredded coconut

2 tablespoons (16 g) acai powder

2 tablespoons (16 g) unsweetened cacao powder

METHOD OF PREPARATION

1 In the bowl of a food processor, add the dates and process until smooth. Transfer to a bowl.

2 Add the walnuts to the food processor and process until finely chopped. Add the cacao powder, hemp seeds, acai powder, and salt. Pulse a couple of times to combine, but do not overmix.

3 Add the dates back to the food processor bowl, along with the nut butter and melted coconut oil. Pulse to combine, resulting in a dough-like mixture.

4 Refrigerate for 10 minutes. Scoop out tablespoons (15 g) and roll into balls. Having slightly wet hands helps this process.

5 Spread the coconut, acai powder, and cacao powder on each of three plates. Roll the balls in the toppings as desired. Transfer to an airtight container and refrigerate until ready to serve.

Acai, Carrot, *and* Zucchini Muffins

MAKES 12 MUFFINS

I love carrot cake and zucchini bread, and these muffins are a combination of both! Hearty and dense, these nutritionally sound muffins are a breakfast, snack, or dessert you can feel good about eating.

INGREDIENTS

1 cup (120 g) all-purpose flour

¼ cup (30 g) acai powder

½ teaspoon baking soda

½ teaspoon baking powder

¾ teaspoon ground cinnamon

¼ teaspoon ground ginger

⅛ teaspoon ground nutmeg

¼ teaspoon kosher salt

¼ cup (50 g) coconut sugar

1 teaspoon vanilla extract

1 tablespoon (15 g) coconut oil, melted

2 large eggs

3 tablespoons (45 ml) unsweetened almond, cashew, or hemp milk

1 cup (110 g) shredded carrot

½ cup (55 g) shredded zucchini

¼ cup (60 g) applesauce

¼ cup (38 g) golden raisins

3 tablespoons (15 g) unsweetened shredded coconut

2 tablespoons (18 g) chopped walnuts

METHOD OF PREPARATION

1 Preheat the oven to 350°F (180°C, or gas mark 4) and line a 12-cup muffin tin with liners; set aside.

2 In a medium bowl, sift together the flour, acai powder, baking soda, baking powder, cinnamon, ginger, nutmeg, and salt; set aside.

3 In another medium bowl, beat together the coconut sugar, vanilla, oil, and eggs until light and creamy. Whisk in the milk.

4 Using a wooden spoon, fold the carrots, zucchini, applesauce, raisins, coconut, and walnuts into the wet ingredients.

5 Add the flour mixture to the wet mixture and stir with the wooden spoon until just incorporated; do not overmix!

6 Spoon the batter into the prepared pan and transfer to the oven. Bake for 22 to 28 minutes, or until a toothpick inserted into the center of one comes out clean. Cool completely on a wire rack.

Acai, Cherry, and Chia Ice Pops

These omega-3, antioxidant-rich ice pops are far better than the store-bought counterparts. They are made a hundred times more nutritious by the inclusion of acai and chia seeds. Feel free to play around with the fruit added. Instead of cherries, you could add blueberries, strawberries, or raspberries.

TIP

Play around with the fruit in these ice pops. If you have an abundance of frozen blueberries, raspberries, blackberries, strawberries, or even peaches . . . change them up and keep cool all summer long.

INGREDIENTS

1 cup (235 ml) unsweetened vanilla-flavored almond milk

2 cups (300 g) frozen organic cherries, pitted

1 frozen banana, peeled

1 tablespoon (8 g) acai powder

3 tablespoons (21 g) chia seeds

METHOD OF PREPARATION

1 Place all the ingredients in a high-powdered blender and blend until smooth.

2 Pour the mixture into ice pop molds and add sticks. Place in the freezer overnight.

3 Unmold and enjoy!

Acai, Chocolate, and Avocado Mousse

SERVES 4

I know, avocado mousse? Sounds strange, but think about the consistency of a ripe avocado—creamy, rich, and delicious—and then add some acai, cacao powder, and peanut butter to the mix and you have a healthy, delicious treat!

TIP

If you prefer frozen custard over mousse, freeze this decadent dessert in individual cups and freeze for a couple of hours. Delicious!

INGREDIENTS

3.5 ounces (100 g) frozen, unsweetened acai puree

1 ripe avocado, halved, peeled, and pitted

¼ cup (30 g) dark unsweetened cacao powder

2 ripe bananas, peeled

2 tablespoons (30 g) chocolate peanut butter

⅓ cup (80 ml) unsweetened vanilla-flavored almond or cashew milk

METHOD OF PREPARATION

1 Run the acai packet under warm water for 10 seconds.

2 Combine the acai, avocado, cacao powder, bananas, chocolate peanut butter, and milk in a high-powered blender. Blend until smooth.

3 Divide among four bowls and serve immediately.

Acai, Chocolate, and Blueberry Cupcakes

MAKES 6 CUPCAKES

These cupcakes are not only delicious but they boast loads of antioxidants. If you can't find or don't have self-rising flour, simply use this substitution: 1 cup (120 g) all-purpose flour + 1½ teaspoons baking powder + ½ teaspoon salt = 1 cup (120 g) self-rising flour.

INGREDIENTS

Cupcakes

1½ cups (300 g) caster sugar

½ cup (112 g) unsalted butter, at room temperature

3 large eggs

½ cup (120 ml) boiling water

1⅔ cups (200 g) self-rising flour

½ cup (60 g) unsweetened dark cacao powder

1 teaspoon baking powder

½ teaspoon kosher salt

Frosting

⅔ cup (150 g) unsalted butter, at room temperature

2½ cups (300 g) confectioner's sugar

3 tablespoons (24 g) acai powder

1 cup (150 g) fresh organic blueberries

METHOD OF PREPARATION

1 To make the cupcakes: Preheat the oven to 350°F (180°C, or gas mark 4). Line 6 cups of a muffin tin with liners; set aside.

2 In a large bowl, mix together the caster sugar and butter using a handheld mixer on medium speed. Mix for 2 minutes, or until fluffy.

3 Add the eggs, one at a time, until incorporated.

4 With the mixer running, slowly add the boiling water until incorporated.

5 In a separate medium bowl, sift together the self-rising flour, cacao powder, baking powder, and salt.

6 Add the flour mixture to the wet ingredients and mix on medium speed until incorporated, 1 to 2 minutes.

7 Spoon the batter evenly into the cupcake liners.

8 Transfer to the oven and bake for 30 to 35 minutes.

9 Remove from the oven and allow to cool in the tin for 10 minutes prior to removing to wire racks to cool completely.

10 To make the frosting: While the cupcakes cool, place the butter in a medium bowl and beat with a handheld mixer on medium speed until pale, light, and fluffy.

11 Slowly add the confectioner's sugar, in about three additions, beating well in between each addition.

12 Add the acai powder and stir to combine.

13 Dollop the buttercream on top of the cooled cupcakes and top with the fresh blueberries.

Blueberry Acai Frozen Yogurt

SERVES 8

This frozen yogurt could not be more simple or refreshing. The addition of lemon zest just makes all the flavors meld and pop! If you want to keep this plant-based, switch the Greek yogurt for coconut yogurt.

INGREDIENTS

1½ cups (360 g) 0% Greek yogurt

¾ cup (150 g) coconut sugar

2 cups (300 g) fresh organic blueberries

7 ounces (200 g) frozen, unsweetened acai puree

2 teaspoons lemon zest

2 teaspoons freshly squeezed lemon juice

METHOD OF PREPARATION

1 In a high-powered blender, combine the yogurt, sugar, blueberries, and acai. Blend until smooth.

2 Pass the mixture through a fine-mesh sieve to remove any seeds.

3 Whisk in the lemon zest and juice.

4 Chill the mixture in the fridge for at least 1 hour.

5 Once chilled, put the mixture into an ice cream maker base and churn for 20 to 30 minutes, or until thick and creamy.

6 Transfer to an airtight container and store in the freezer until ready to eat.

No-bake
Acai, Himalayan Pink Salt, Date, and Dark Cacao Fudge

MAKES 16 PIECES

No-bake desserts are the best and a great way to have your kids help out in the kitchen. These treats are salty-sweet exceptional fudgy goodness. Cacao butter and paste can normally be found at any health food store or ordered online.

INGREDIENTS

½ cup (60 g) acai powder

3 tablespoons (45 g) coconut oil

10 soft Medjool dates, pitted

½ cup (60 g) almond flour

1 teaspoon pink Himalayan sea salt, divided

1 cup (225 g) cacao butter

1 cup (225 g) cacao paste

¼ cup (60 ml) maple syrup

1 teaspoon vanilla extract

½ cup (70 g) raw pumpkin seeds (optional)

METHOD OF PREPARATION

1 Line an 8 x 8-inch (20 x 20-cm) baking dish with parchment paper; set aside.

2 Combine the acai powder, coconut oil, dates, almond flour, and ¼ teaspoon of the sea salt in the bowl of a food processor. Process until the dates are well incorporated and the mixture is smooth. Transfer to a bowl and set aside.

3 In a small saucepan over medium heat, add the cacao butter and cacao paste and melt for 2 to 3 minutes.

4 Remove from the heat and add the maple syrup, vanilla, and ¼ teaspoon of the sea salt. Whisk until incorporated; stir in the pumpkin seeds, if using.

5 Pour half of the chocolate mixture into the prepared pan.

6 Shape the acai mixture in your hands to fit the shape of the brownie pan and lay it on top of the bottom layer of chocolate. Pour the remainder of the chocolate on top of the acai layer. Sprinkle with the remaining ½ teaspoon salt.

7 Transfer the fudge to the freezer and freeze for at least 45 minutes to 1 hour.

8 Cut into 16 squares and serve.

INDEX